For Johannes Felix – welcome to the world

Visit Catherine and Laurence Anholt's website at
www.anholt.co.uk

ORCHARD BOOKS
338 Euston Road, London NWI 3BH
Orchard Books Australia
Level 17/207 Kent Street, Sydney, NSW 2000

First published in 2011 by Orchard Books
First published in paperback in 2012

ISBN 978 1 40831 169 1

Text © Laurence Anholt 2011
Illustrations © Catherine Anholt 2011
The rights of Laurence Anholt to be identified as the author
and Catherine Anholt to be identified as the illustrator of this work
have been asserted by them in accordance with the
Copyright, Designs and Patents Act, 1988.

A CIP catalogue record for this book
is available from the British Library.

1 3 5 7 9 10 8 6 4 2
Printed in China

Orchard Books is a division of Hachette Children's Books,
an Hachette UK company.
www.hachette.co.uk

WE L♥VE BEARS

Catherine and Laurence Anholt

ORCHARD

Look! There's a bear on my chair,
he's sitting there brushing his hair.

He said, "It's my favourite day,
when the teddy bears come out to play."

So we slid down the stairs with our bear,
there was porridge and honey to share.

Our bear said, "I know what you'll like, come and ride with a bear on a bike."

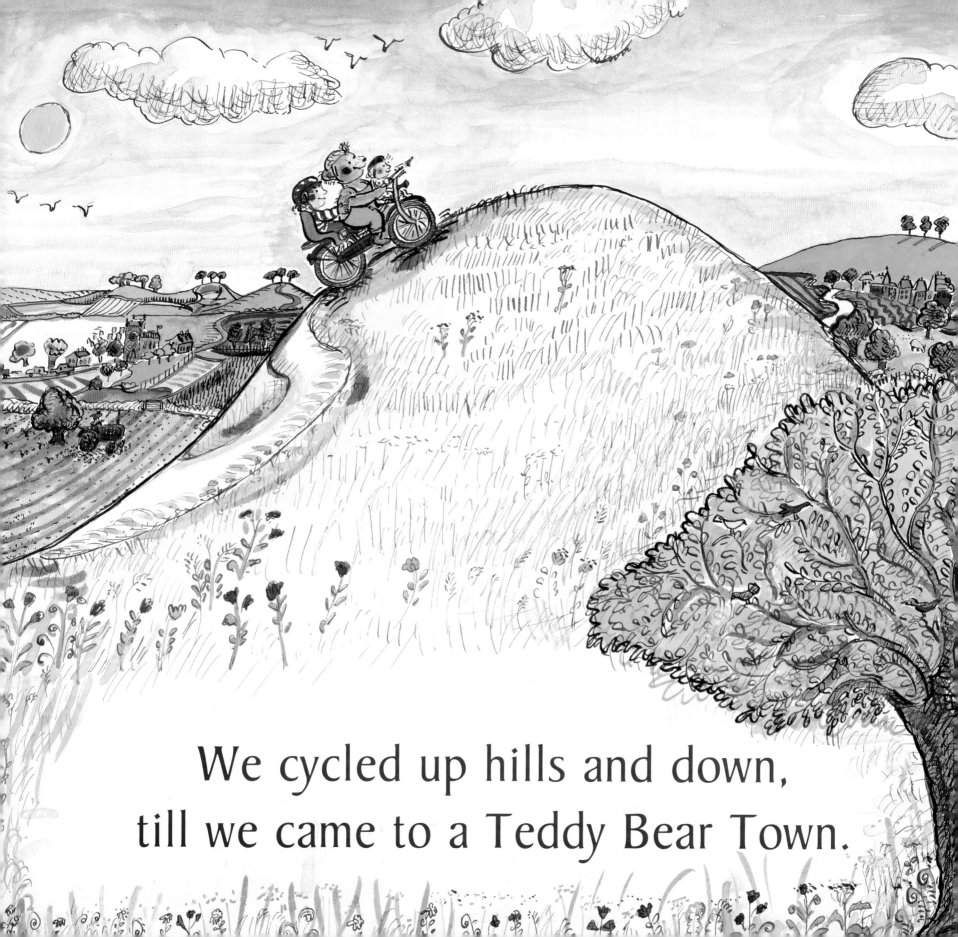

We cycled up hills and down,
till we came to a Teddy Bear Town.

We each held his teddy bear paw,
and we couldn't believe what we saw . . .

There were hundreds and thousands of bears,
talking and walking in pairs.

There were teddy bears dressed up in skirts,
and pyjamas and trousers and shirts.

There were teddy bears riding in trains,
and tractors and diggers and planes.

Then we ran with our bear everywhere,
to a pool and a school and a fair.

As he patted his big bear tummy,
our bear said, "I'd like something yummy."

So we went to each shop in the street,
and we chose lots of good things to eat.

We bought milk shakes and chocolate ice cream, this candyfloss tastes like a dream!

Our bear ate a box of bananas,
and some sandwiches full of sultanas.

Our bear said, "Now, this is our chance, we can go to the Teddy Bear Dance."

Get ready! Get steady! Let's jump,
we can bump to the teddy bear thump.

Then our teddy was ready to go,
"I feel rather tired, you know."

As the sun went down in the sky,
all the bears in the town waved goodbye.

So we climbed in a big balloon,
and floated home under the moon.
That was our favourite day,
when the teddy bears came out to play.

The stars shone down on the path,
and our bear took us up for a bath.

As he tucked us up tightly in bed,
"We love you, dear teddy," we said.